COPY NO. 2

D0526506

WITHDRAWN FROM THE POETRY LIBRARY

Poems for Pensioners

Andy Seed is a writer and humourist based in North Yorkshire. He's the author of over 30 books including the popular 'All Teachers' trilogy of memoirs for adults and a range of titles for children, including *The Silly Book of Side-Splitting Stuff* – winner of the 2015 Blue Peter Book Award – and the acclaimed funny children's novel *Prankenstein*.

Poems for Pensioners

Andy Seed

with illustrations by
Scott Garrett

POETRY LIBRARY
SOUTHBANK CENTRE
ROYAL FESTIVAL HALL
LONDON SE1 8XX
VP

Valley Press

First published in 2016 by Valley Press
Woodend, The Crescent, Scarborough, YO11 2PW
www.valleypressuk.com

First edition, first printing (August 2016)

ISBN 978-1-908853-72-1
Cat. no. VP0089

Copyright © Andy Seed 2016
www.andyseed.com

The right of Andy Seed to be identified as the
author of this work has been asserted in accordance with
the Copyright, Designs and Patents Act 1988.

All rights reserved. No part of this publication may be
reproduced, stored in or introduced into a retrieval system,
or transmitted in any form, by any means (electronic,
mechanical, photocopying, recording or otherwise) without
prior written permission from the rights holders.

A CIP record for this book is available from the British Library.

Printed and bound in the EU by Pulsio, Paris.

Contents

To Eddie and Wendy,
pensioners of supreme loveliness

What did I walk into this room for?

What did I walk into this room for?
Was it to feed the cat?
Well, since I haven't got one,
It probably wasn't that.

What did I walk into this room for?
Was it something to do with beef?
Well, I couldn't eat it anyway,
As I'm short of twenty-eight teeth.

What did I walk into this room for?
Was it to clean the sink?
Well, since I'm in the garage,
It wasn't that, I think.

What did I walk into this room for?
Was it to pick up a saw?
Yes it was – it's all coming back now!
Right ... what do I need it for?

Always Read the Label

No wonder
You're still
On the
Toilet, Dilys;
Remember
The pills
That were blue?
You were
Supposed to
Take two
Every twenty-four hours,
Not twenty-four
Every two.

Nursing Home Bet

This is what happened,
One Friday in May,
At the nursing home,
With your Great Aunt Faye.

She was sitting in the lounge,
When a gent shuffled by,
With braces and a waistband,
Remarkably high.

'I bet you a pound,'
Said Faye to this chum,
'I can tell your age,
Just by looking at your bum.'

'Right, you're on,' said the gent,
Loosening his braces,
'Although people usually
Go by faces.'

Faye took a glance
At the wrinkly rear,
'Ninety-two,' she announced,
'Am I near?'

'Amazing!' he declared,
'Precisely right –
How do you do it?
Is it second sight?'

'Not second sight exactly,'
Hooted Aunt Faye,
'I was at your birthday party
Just yesterday.'

Care Home Crises

Nellie's in love with Arthur,
But Arthur has taken to Faye;
Faye has eyes only for Norman,
But Norman's devoted to Kaye.

Kaye really longs for Harold,
Harold is trying to woo Betty,
While Betty's besotted with Maurice,
And Maurice has fallen for Nettie.

Nettie is partial to Frank,
Though Frank's an admirer of Doreen;
Doreen's enamoured with Victor,
But Victor cares only for Maureen.

Maureen? Well she adores Cyril,
Yet Cyril is smitten with Nellie;
I suppose we're back where we started;
Forget love – let's go and watch telly.

Upgrading Granny

Granny's been to the hospital.
She needed an upgrade again;
Her body's been stripped and refitted
By an army of white-coated men.

Her new teeth are pure carbon fibre,
Her specs were designed with a laser;
She can now bite through plates if she wants to
And her eyesight's as sharp as a razor.

She's got digital hearing aid power,
And her pacemaker's nuclear I'm told;
They replaced her hip with a stainless steel joint
And her Zimmer's now radio controlled.

There was a special offer on memory,
She got 64 megs of it free;
She can now recall where she left granddad
And that I owe her 35p.

Her toilet's controlled by computer,
Her electric shopping cart's fun;
Her stairlift's got internet access –
I can't wait till I'm ninety-one...

A Visit from Great Granny

We can always tell
When great granny has been,
There are tablets
All over the bed;
There are bloomers
Inside the dishwasher
And no one
Can find the bread.

We can always tell
When great granny has been,
In the fridge
We'll notice a hat;
There's an armchair
In front of the microwave
And the budgie's been fed –
To the cat.

Where I Played When I was Young

Where the grass was soft and long,
Where the river drifts along,
Where the meadow pipits sang,
Where the gentle bluebells sprang,

Where the farmyard hay was stacked,
Where strings of polished chestnuts cracked,
Where the stooping heron fished,
Where plans and dreams and hopes were wished,

Where the bridge held back the pool,
Where the crags and heather ruled,
Where the woods grew deep and free,
Where the hills spied out the sea,

Where we watched the brown hare run,
Where orchards caught the evening sun,
Where boughs of rosy apples hung;
That's where I played when I was young.

Bus Pass

I've finally got me pension,
I've decided to sell me car,
It's free travel for me from this day on,
I'm going to go really far.

So I stood there at the bus stop,
With my arm out bold as brass,
The Number 14 came along,
And
    I
       watched
          the
            bus
              pass.

My Neighbours

I don't know my neighbours any more,
And sadly they don't know me;
I've no idea who lives next door
At number 23.

It could be a spy or an opera star,
Or a writer of purple prose;
I only know that she drives a Ford
And has a sparkly thing in her nose.

The family who live across the road
Have thirty-five kids (so it seems);
Their life is a circular unending rush
Of taxiing toddlers and teens.

The man who lives at number 18
Takes his dog for walks;
I pass him when I go to the shops
And receive a nod, but no talk.

There are two young students at number 15,
I certainly know when they're in;
Their music booms out right across the estate,
They only play one type: din.

The people at 10 are also loud,
Bawling and arguing so;
But none of them ever opens their mouth
To say the word 'hello'.

Mrs Jones is scared to go out,
Bob at 19 works all hours;
There's a retired gardener chap just moved in,
But he won't chat to people, just flowers.

So much has changed in this corner of town,
Where I've lived since the summer of '73;
But I don't know my neighbours any more,
And, sadly, they don't know me.

When you get older

When you get older,
Hardly anything works,
Except for the things
That really hurt.

When you get older,
You may be retired,
But there are no days off –
You can't even get fired.

When you get older,
You abandon modern culture
And just feed the birds –
Are those circling vultures?

When you get older,
There are a few pluses;
You're given a bus pass –
Shame there's no buses.

When you get older,
All the sitting is boring;
Your bottom falls asleep –
I can hear mine snoring.

When you get older,
Milky cereals you chew
But the snap, crackle, pop
Only comes from you.

When you get older,
You call your sister Jane,
Which would be alright
If that were her name.

When you get older,
They call you trouble maker;
One with influence diminished –
Not a mover but a shaker.

When you get older,
Time goes so fast;
You can't keep up –
So you live in the past.

When you get older,
You do tend to snore,
And you miss a lot of things –
But you've seen it all before.

Oh Dear Doctor Johnson

Oh dear
Doctor Johnson,
My eyesight's
Getting worse.

I fear you
May be right there –
This is the library,
Mrs Hurst.

QUIET PLEASE

A New Man

First old grandad's teeth went,
Then he lost his hair;
His eyesight was the next to go,
A gent in disrepair.

He needed a hip replacement then,
And two new knees 'n' all;
Oh, and a couple of grafted corneas
At the back of each eyeball.

He was waiting for an aortic valve
For his very dicky heart;
Plus a pair of working kidneys
And sixteen other parts.

The docs took a look at granddad,
And hatched a crafty plan;
They decided to transplant *all* of him –
He's now a brand new man.

BHS *(Before Health and Safety)*

We swam in rivers,
Fell out of trees,
Jumped off the bus
And skinned our knees.

We hid in the woods,
Fished in lakes,
Raced on bikes
With dodgy brakes.

We played near ponds,
On building sites;
Crossed busy roads,
Flew our own kites.

Throwing snowballs
For winter thrills;
Sliding on ice,
Sledging down hills.

Building tree houses,
Dens with sticks;
Making go karts,
Learning tricks.

With catapults, penknives,
Arrows and bows;
Stings and splinters,
Bloodied nose.

Armed with stink bombs,
Or itching powder;
Jumping Jacks,
Or something louder.

We ate cakes and cream
And toffee and jam,
Pilfered apples
And tins of spam.

We drank from glass bottles,
Had lead-paint toys;
And were whacked by teachers
When naughty boys.

There were no bike helmets,
No childproof lids;
No mobile phones,
Just happy kids.

Tech-no-thanks

I want nothing to do with Facebook
And what on earth is Twitter?
I'm happy with my woolly socks
And half a pint of bitter.

Someone gave me a mobile phone
But I couldn't record a greeting –
Well, it took me nearly seven years
To work the central heating!

Now it's online this and website that
But I'm scared to go on the net;
I don't want a computer,
Just give me some winceyette.

I haven't a clue what an iPad does
(Or is it an iPod? No idea!)
And why would I need an iPhone?
Surely a phone's for your ear...

About Xboxes, Playstations, Nintendos,
I really am not worried,
And if I need a Wii I'll go for one,
But it certainly won't be at Currys.

Day to Forget

Went to the shops,
Forgot my list,
Bought some chocolate,
Couldn't resist.
Got to the till,
Forgot my purse,
Had no money,
Then it got worse.
Began to walk home,
Forgot the car,
Luckily hadn't
Got very far.
Looked for the car,
Forgot where I'd parked,
Was it at Tesco or
Marks and Sparks?
Found the car,
But forgot to get fuel,
Stopped at the garage
Next to the school.
Filled it up,
Forgot my purse,
Now things were really
Getting worse.

They asked my address,
Forgot my street,
I heard the approach
Of a siren's beat.
'Name?' said the policeman,
'I've forgotten,' I said,
He took out the handcuffs,
Away I was led.
And then I woke up,
In the chair by the hall,
And as for the dream?
I've forgotten it all.

Cold Call Calamity

Stop
Stop
STOP!

Stop
Ringing me!

I don't want your...

Insurance quotes,
Council votes,

PPI,
Sport from Sky,

Accident claims,
Window frames,

Broadband deals,
Charity appeals,

Stupid shares,
Flimsy wares,

Timeshare villa,
Save the gorilla,

Lottery malarkey,
Replacement car key,

Cash from Nigeria,
Cures for diphtheria,

Rubbish free trials,
Or those cushions for piles –

So stop ringing me
You horrible person!

Oh, sorry,
It's you mother.

Crisps for a Pound

Yesterday at the railway station,
I saw crisps for a pound –
What's become
Of this nation?

Crisps for a pound?
Has the world gone mad?
A pound was a fortune,
When I was a lad.

A pound would buy a train set,
Or a decent coat,
A second-hand bike,
A good model boat.

You could have roller skates,
And a pile of books,
Or a fishing rod
With bait and hooks.

A quid was a scooter,
A leather ball,
Or a one-man tent,
As I recall.

Twenty bob
For a packet of what?
Salty potatoes
Fried in grot.

So I got water instead,
Then stood in the line
And cried when the girl said,
One ninety-nine.

It's Rude to Stare

Staring at mobiles
While they eat,
In front of the telly,
Crossing the street.

Staring at mobiles
Stood in a queue,
In the shops,
On the loo.

Staring at mobiles
With friends in a bar,
In the cinema,
Driving a car.

Staring at mobiles
Making the tea,
Riding a bike,
Ignoring me.

Conversation with My Granddaughter

So Nana
Told you
She's a
Younger tart?

I think
The phrase
You want
Is 'young at heart'.

Choose a Cruise

(With acknowledgments to Frida Wolfe)

Blue cruise, red cruise,
Maybe round the Med cruise.
Tell me what would you choose
If we had the dough?

Posh cruise, dosh cruise,
Lots-of-lovely-nosh cruise,
Sparkly spray-and-wash cruise;
I really want to go.

Sun cruise, fun cruise,
Everything-is-done cruise,
A competition-won cruise;
That's the one for me.

BUT

Slow cruise, no cruise,
None-of-us-can-go cruise,
Here's-an-oar-and-row cruise;
That's what it'll be.

Bill's Pills

I can't play outside
With the grandkids, Flo.
I'd best stay here
In the building.

It's those pills
I got from the doctor, dear.
They say
'Keep away from children'.

Grandchildren

Full of smiles, full of rush,
Endless questions, little hush;

Lots of laughter, lots of games,
Naughty noises, silly names;

Calls for telly, calls for treats,
Disney films and sticky sweets;

Out in the garden, out to the park,
Sliding, climbing, swinging arc;

Choosing stories, sharing books,
Cosy snuggles, sleepy looks;

Tired out, tucked in the sack,
It's lovely to have them – and give them back.

My Grandson

The attention span
Of a mayfly's blink;
Only eats chips
And fizzy drinks.

Everything is loud
And bish bosh bash,
And requires a stream
Of ready cash.

Half watches TV
While playing a game
On some infernal device
(I don't know its name).

Doesn't read books;
Doesn't say please;
Doesn't have grazes
On his knees.

If I tell him off
He cries for his mum;
In my day
He'd've got a smacked bum.

Gives me cheek
Though I tower above him;
What a scamp –
Good job I love him.

Another Day

I make a cup of tea;
Stroke the cat;
Watch a bit of telly;
Dust the flat.

Walk to the shops;
Make some toast;
Do a little ironing;
Check the post.

Have a sit down;
Take a snooze;
Read the paper;
Clean my shoes.

I'm independent
With my iPad and phone;
In good health,
And all alone.

Beryl and Arthur Meet in the Park

How's yer gout?

Oh fine, it's nowt.

The corns giving gyp?

No not really, zip.

Still got that rash?

Be gone in a flash.

Any better yer back?

Nothing wrong says me quack.

Are those bunions still sore?

Not as bad as before.

I heard you 'ad shingles.

Ha, barely tingles.

Yer blood pressure high?

Oh, you know, I get by.

Constipation okay?

                    No trouble today!

Did that piles cream work?

                    Huh, drove me beserk.

Oh well, look after yerself.

                    Just as well I've got me health.

 Poetry Library

I Was On My Way

I was on the way
To wash the floor
When I saw the post
Inside the door;
I picked up a statement
From the bank
And remembered that cheque
From Cousin Frank
That wasn't paid in
So I went to the file
Which was underneath
An enormous pile
Upon the desk
Where I left the cheque
But forgot to pick up
My reading specs,
So I fetched the glasses
From my coat
And that's when I found
A scribbled note
To buy some milk –
I completely forgot!
So I put on my shoes
To walk to the shop;
But as I found my bag
To get some money

I detected the smell
Of something funny;
The kitchen bin
Was turning high
With mouldy cheese
And old fish pie,
So I took it outside
But on the way
I noticed some weeds
In the border display,
So I pulled them out,
Stifled a yawn,
Headed back inside
When I saw the lawn –
It was very dry and bare and grey
So I went for some water
But on the way
I noticed a mug
Left out by Jack –
Oh why can't people
Put things back?
So I took it inside
Just through the door
And that's when I noticed
The kitchen floor –
That needs a wash;
Best take off my rings –
It's a good job that *someone*
Gets on with things.

Doris was a Knitter

Doris was a knitter
And she'd knit, knit, knit;
She always knitted jumpers
Which didn't fit, fit, fit.

Doris was a knitter
And she'd knit, knit, knit;
She never used a pattern
Not a bit, bit, bit.

Doris was a knitter
And she'd knit, knit, knit;
Scarves so long you'd trip up
Like a twit, twit, twit.

Doris was a knitter
And she'd knit, knit, knit;
Now she's gone I miss her
Quite a bit, bit, bit.

Epitaphs

Here is Tim,
Who went
To the gym;
Alas, discovered
It didn't
Suit him.

Here lies Iris,
Former nurse;
Along the M6
She reversed.

Rest in peace
'Windy' Ron
(It's much more peaceful
Now you're gone).

Here lies the body
Of Mary Dinnings,
Who spent all of
Her bingo winnings
On Pink Champagne,
Carefully picked;
It came in the bucket
Which Mary kicked.

In memory
Of Eric, engineer;
Souped up
His stairlift;
Oh dear.

Here is buried
Godfrey Hunt –
Put his teeth in
Back to front.

Here lies
Henrietta Speke;
Didn't feed
Her cats
One week.

Sacred to the memory
Of whatsis name.

Gone but not forgotten

(Memories of growing up in the 1950s and before)

Climbing trees and playing in the street,
Going to the pictures at two bob a seat;
Fishing for tiddlers, British bulldog,
Postman's knock, hiding in the smog.

Out down the road to the corner shop,
For barley sugar and bottles of pop;
Dandelion and burdock, Victory Vees,
Condensed milk and tins of peas.

Next door's telly had Muffin the Mule,
Laurel and Hardy playing the fool;
Roy Rodgers, The Woodentops,
Buster Keaton and the Keystone Cops.

Down in the yard with clockwork toys,
Dolls for girls and catapults for boys;
Some had Hornby with oval tracks,
Others had marbles, tiddlywinks, jacks.

Home for tea with dripping on toast,
Or salty gravy with Sunday roast;
Pale blancmange, spotted dick,
Or tapioca pudding, lumpy and thick.

Winter's dark with wireless tunes,
Family Favourites or giggling with The Goons;
Dick Barton chases, The Clitheroe Kid,
Or Hancock's Half Hour with Tony and Sid.

No seat belts for seaside trips,
Bucket and spade, fish and chips;
Knitted swimming suits and sandy knees,
Butlins camps and freezing seas.

Cod liver oil, kaleidoscopes,
Wooden mangles and coal tar soap;
National Service, Ovaltine,
Measles, mumps and gaberdines.

Steam and coal at railway stations,
Prefabs and the Coronation,
Vim and Omo, trotters and tripe,
Helter skelters and smoky pipes.

Gone but not forgotten, I see them all,
With names and faces I recall;
Life was different in many ways,
I'm grateful for those happy days.

Packet In

A Christmas present from my wife
Was a sleek electric carving knife,
It needed batteries in the back,
So I walked to the shops and bought a pack.

It was a plastic bubble with cardboard backing,
The packet as always took some cracking;
I twisted it, bent it, pulled it hard,
That weapons-grade plastic and bulletproof card.

I took off my jumper, stretched my neck,
Would it open? Would it heck!
No lid, no notch, no opening flap,
No perforations, no hint to unwrap.

So next I tried scissors and they did make a nick,
But the PVC armour was sturdy and thick.
Muttering and cursing I reached for a cleaver,
By now I was sweating with packaging fever.
I chopped and I cut, I poked and I panned,
But only succeeded in slicing my hand.

'Right!' I growled and stomped to the shed.
'I'm getting the toolbox: prepare to be dead.'
I stabbed it with screwdrivers, hit it with awls,
Yanked it with pliers and sawed it with saws,
But that little clear package remained tightly shut,
While my fingers were bloody with grazes and cuts.

Enough is enough! I've looked like a fool,
But I have an ace, a new power tool:
The electric knife! Now my temper was fired;
There was just one problem: *Four batteries required.*

Never Again

Cuthbert first tried online shopping,
For Brasso and sliced Mother's Pride;
But when he switched off the computer,
He had four timeshares
And an internet bride.

Cuthbert's now always on holiday,
With Olga there at his side,
She's nineteen, blonde and long-legged;
But he'd still rather have
Mother's Pride.

Whatever

Dedicated to 'those in peril on the seat'
(who would hear the call of nature if they'd
remembered to put their hearing aid in).

Whatever the season, whatever the light,
Whatever the phase of the moon;
Whatever the time of day or night,
My life is ruled by the prune.

Whether I'm in or whether I'm out,
Whether in Hull or Rangoon;
Whether there's flood or whether there's drought,
My life is ruled by the prune.

If I'm with friend or if I'm with foe,
If I'm with tramp or tycoon;
If I'm advising the Mayor of Bordeaux,
My life is ruled by the prune.

Whatever hope brings, whatever my fate,
Whatever I rant or impugn;
Whatever my inner spiritual state,
My life is ruled by the prune.

Tea at the Vicar's

Ethel put
Her best
Clothes on,
When invited
For tea
At the vicar's;

It's a shame
That no one
Told her that
Her dress
Was caught up
In her
Knickers.

Hairy Tales

(An elderly gent's struggle)

My noggin has given up the fight,
Gravity's won the day;
The hair that once grew up on my head
Now comes down through my nostrils like hay.

My bonce is a smooth and shiny dome,
It's been like that for years;
I can understand why my eyebrows are bushy,
But who needs hairs in their ears?

No wonder I'm so hard of hearing,
There's a jungle in each lug!
I think I'll collect all the trimmings
And wear the resultant rug.

Let Bygones be Bygones

We went to see the folk museum
At Hutton-on-the-Hill;
I thought the café very good,
Until I got the bill.

We toured the exhibition rooms
And the demonstration crafts;
Although the guide there spoke to us
As if we were slightly daft.

'How We Once Lived' was the final display,
And here I had a grouse;
The 'traditional home' with bygones on show
Was just the same as my house!

That Boy I Went to School With

That boy I went to school with
Is old and lined and grey;
He has the same persuasive smile
That once led me astray.

That boy I went to school with
Is frail and small and slow,
And yet the years have not changed this:
That boy is still my beau.

Sight for Sore Eyes

Betty's eyes went
Slowly downhill,
But she never complained
To her husband Bill.

Her world became cloudy,
But like a good wife
She just muddled through
And got on with life.

Reading became harder,
Driving a bind;
Her outlook turned grey
As she slowly went blind.

Bill took her hand saying,
'This has to stop.'
And their doctor arranged
For a cataract op.

It was simple and painless,
Remarkably brief;
Betty came home
With hope and belief.

And gradually objects
Came into view
As Betty's new eyes
Disclosed what was true.

Betty saw colours
As they should be seen:
Vivid and vibrant
Yellows and greens.

She turned to the mirror
And checked what she wore:
A beret of olive,
A coat of azure.

Her first words to Bill
As she took off her hat?
'HOW DID YOU LET ME
GO OUT WEARING THAT!'

The Cycling Club Reunion

In our 30s we met in York,
We loved its many pubs.

In our 40s we met in York,
For the waitresses in the clubs.

In our 50s we met in York,
For the food at the quiet B&B.

In our 60s we met in York,
For all the history to see.

In our 70s we met in York,
For the wheelchair-friendly tours.

In our 80s we met in York,
Cos we'd never been there before.

Retirement

A question's been bothering me all night long;
I really must enquire:
What on earth do gardeners do
When they decide to retire?

Things That Cheer Me

The verges in spring,
A child on a swing.

A cat on my lap,
An afternoon nap.

Freshly baked bread,
A sunset of red.

The song of a thrush,
The countryside's hush.

A baby's soft cheek,
A polished antique.

Old photographs,
Infectious laughs.

The sway of the trees,
A warm summer breeze.

A hug from a friend,
A family weekend.

A view of the sea,
And a good cup of tea.

What Counts

It's not the greying hair,
It's not the missing teeth,
It's not the crumpled skin,
    It's the person underneath.

It's not the groaning joints,
It's not the fading eyes,
It's not the memory loss,
    It's the person deep inside.

It's not the walking stick,
It's not a bandage nor a scar,
It's not the outer things,
    It's the person that you are.

Acknowledgments

Many thanks to all those people who encouraged me to write this book (in some cases before I had even thought about it), in particular to Joyce Hodgson and her lovely and lively 'Young at Heart' group.

I'd also like to pass on my gratitude to the residents of Princess Court in Malton for their tremendous ideas, and to others who gave invaluable help, not least my ever-smart in-laws Trevor and Lisette Osbourn for their wealth of suggestions.

Finally, a generous thanks to my editor and publisher Jamie McGarry for his enthusiasm and good old Yorkshire nous.